true love
PROJECT

40 DAYS
OF PURITY
FOR GUYS

Clayton King

B&H
PUBLISHING GROUP
Nashville, Tennessee

978-1-4336-8435-7

Published by B&H Publishing Group
Nashville, Tennessee

Dewey Decimal Classification: 306.73
Subject Heading: BOYS \ SEXUAL ABSTINENCE \
CHRISTIAN LIFE

1 2 3 4 5 6 • 18 17 16 15 14

This book is dedicated to Joe and Jane King, my parents who adopted me when I was just a few weeks old. They didn't have a perfect marriage, but they stayed faithful to Christ and to each other all the way until death. They taught me more about love through their example than I could learn from a thousand books.

Contents

40 DAYS OF PURITY

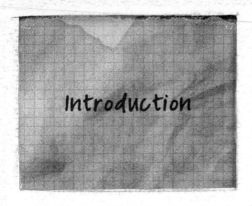

Introduction

The task of living your life for the glory of God is a tremendous challenge for any Christian. It's even more difficult in a culture that shoves sex, porn, and lust in your face incessantly. Add to that the daily, even hourly struggle of trying to avoid sexual temptation, and it can at times seem nearly impossible.

The truth is, it is impossible . . . if you try to do it on your own.

It is impossible . . . if you don't understand **why** you should live according to God's plan.

It is impossible . . . if you don't know **how** to stand against the tide.

1

It is impossible . . . if you don't understand *what* you should do in your fight for holiness and godliness.

It is impossible . . . if you don't know *who* you are and *whom* you belong to.

So we're going to learn how to do this together, day-by-day. We're going to see what God says in regards to giving your entire life, not just your relationships, to Him. We will figure out how to live your life on purpose based on who you are and who God is making you to be. You will see that it's not too hard. It's not too complicated. It's not impossible.

If you belong to Jesus Christ, His Spirit is in you, He is with you, and He is for you. And He has a greater purpose for your life than you could ever imagine.

chosen

But you are a chosen race, a royal priesthood, a holy nation, a people for His possession, so that you may proclaim the praises of the One who called you out of darkness into His marvelous light. Once you were not a people, but now you are God's people; you had not received mercy, but now you have received mercy.

—1 PETER 2:9–10

My life seemed fairly simple as a kid. Then I started middle school.

Everything changed: my body, my desires, my thoughts, and my attention. I had always thought girls were gross. Then all of a sudden, they were all I could think about. And I wasn't alone. My guy friends were going through a similar metamorphosis; so were all the girls we secretly dreamed about. This led to a new form of entertainment: *relationships*.

Guys started flirting with girls, and girls started whispering about guys. What I once found disgusting suddenly became an obsession. All I wanted was a girlfriend! A girl would make me confident, secure, and cool. I would become one of the guys and be accepted by them if I could just get a girl to like me. I desperately hoped I would be chosen by a cute girl because that would validate me as a guy.

But as the days became weeks and the weeks became months, not a single girl chose to like me. I became more self-conscious and more insecure. I wondered how I was going to convince a girl to like me when I wasn't even sure if I liked myself. I was trying to fill the natural human desire to be noticed, to find affection and love through a relationship, but I kept coming up empty. I was emotionally vulnerable and spiritually insecure.

Middle school turned into high school, and I grew a foot and lost forty pounds and became a football player. Girls began to notice me, and a few of them even chose to *like* me. It made me feel awesome for a little while, but I felt a deeper longing inside my heart. **The security I hoped a girlfriend would bring me never came. I realized that only Jesus could fulfill my longing to matter, to belong, and to be chosen by someone.**

If you know that the God of the universe chose you to be His child, why would you ever let another person define who you are or who you will become?

When you're tempted to base your identity on a relationship, remember that Jesus gave up His life to give yours value. If a girl likes you one day only to reject you the next, remember Jesus' love doesn't flip-flop. He is consistent. He is faithful, and His love is eternal.

Girls, dating, drama, and relationships are here today and gone tomorrow, but Jesus is the one consistent love you can always count on, no matter what. You've been chosen by God. Will you choose to make your relationship with Jesus the most important one in your life? You have a choice. Make the right one.

DAY 2

The Challenge

Let us run with endurance the race that lies before us, keeping our eyes on Jesus, the source and perfecter of our faith.

—HEBREWS 12:1–2

Most of us have been told that Jesus' love is unconditional and permanent. But the test of whether we really believe it comes in those moments when we feel like we've failed Jesus. All of a sudden the door of doubt opens in our hearts, and uneasy thoughts creep in. **We doubt His love when we break His laws**.

The more we doubt, the farther we run from the truth that's promised to us in Scripture: He loves us faithfully even when we are not faithful. The challenge is to believe this is true, even when all our feelings and emotions cause us to question it.

We tend to adopt a subtle attitude. We assume God would be impressed with us if we could do more good deeds, if we could keep more of His commandments, or if we could stop sinning completely. But we all know this is impossible.

In the book of Matthew, Jesus talks to a group of religious leaders. These guys thought keeping the law earned them brownie points with God. Jesus said to them, "Woe to you, scribes and Pharisees, hypocrites! You are like whitewashed tombs, which appear beautiful on the outside, but inside are full of dead men's bones and every impurity" (Matthew 23:27). The Pharisees knew that God's law required perfect obedience so they created rules and laws that made them feel they were keeping the law perfectly. Just like us, they were trying to live up to an impossible standard. It's as if Jesus were saying to them, "Hey guys, you may think all these good things you are doing are throwing Me off, but nothing is invisible to Me. I wish you'd stop trying to impress Me and start trusting Me."

If you're trying to perfect yourself, you're taking on a job only Jesus can accomplish. Your perfection is a by-product of your salvation. He's already made you perfect even though you may not feel like it today.

When my first girlfriend broke up with me, I thought my life was over. I questioned what I could have done differently. I wondered what was wrong with me and if another girl would ever like me. But my dad spoke wisdom to me when he said, "Son, you're not perfect, and a good girl will love you for who you really are. She won't expect you to be perfect. And neither does God."

When I fail and I'm frustrated, I thank Jesus that one day He will remove all shame, and He'll welcome me into His kingdom, *not based on my performance but on His perfection.* The challenge is to believe God still loves and cherishes you when your performance is less than perfect. And since it is always less than perfect, this will be a challenge you will face for the rest of your life.

Accept the challenge. Remember that God doesn't love you because you are perfect. He loves you perfectly because He is perfect.

The Choice

Give, and it will be given to you; a good measure—pressed down, shaken together, and running over—will be poured into your lap. For with the measure you use, it will be measured back to you.

—LUKE 6:38

The most important choice you'll ever make when it comes to sexual purity is not whom you will date or how far you will go physically. All of those choices are important, but they are not ultimate.

The greatest choice you'll ever make is whether you will give absolute, total, complete, irreversible control of your life to Jesus Christ. Will you hold anything back from Him?

I know how it feels to fear that giving up control of every part of your life to Jesus may mean He will keep something good from you. Who would want to give up their sexual desires to God if He won't ever let you have sex (or a girlfriend or a wife or any fun)?

So when you're trying to make the choice totally to surrender control of your life to Jesus, remember a few things:

1. You can't choose *whom you will love* until you decide *who is Lord.* No girl on this earth can fully complete you, satisfy you, and make you happy for a lifetime. She would have to be God to do that. And that's the point. Only God can give you all you need and desire in life. God—not romance or relationships—is the ultimate pursuit. Choose to make Him the Lord of your life, your Boss, Master, Ruler, and King.

2. You can't choose *what you will do* until you decide *who you are*. Thousands of guys over the last twenty-five years have asked me: "How far is too far with a girl? What am I allowed to do physically before marriage?" But those are not the right questions. You have to choose what kind of man you are. Are you a man of conviction? integrity? honesty? Are you trustworthy? hardworking? dependable? Are you a man of God who is pursuing Jesus with all your heart?

3. You can't choose *whom you'll become* until you decide *what you believe*. Most guys have similar dreams for what they want out of life. They want to become successful. Marry a nice girl. Have a family. Make some money. Own a nice house. Travel and go on cool vacations. Be respected by their friends. Yet these things will prove meaningless in the long run if you don't know what you believe about Jesus, life, marriage, commitment, raising children, and the church. We always become what we believe.

If you choose to keep control of any area of your life, you will regret it because you're not smart enough to be Lord. However, if you choose to give Jesus complete control of your life, He will bless you beyond your wildest dreams. Choose now to trust Jesus with everything, including your sexual purity.

Give Him everything.

The Hard Work of Holiness

Not that I have already reached the goal or am already fully mature, but I make every effort to take hold of it because I also have been taken hold of by Christ Jesus. Brothers, I do not consider myself to have taken hold of it. But one thing I do: Forgetting what is behind and reaching forward to what is ahead, I pursue as my goal the prize promised by God's heavenly call in Christ Jesus.

—Philippians 3:12–14

My son's first football season was hilarious. The boys ranged in age from five to eight. Some of them could barely run in their pads, and it was next to impossible for the coach to keep their attention. How do you get a bunch of boys to focus when they can hardly see past their enormous helmets? You teach them a chant, of course! It went like this: "HARD WORK . . . PAYS OFF!"

The idea wasn't original, but it was genius. Somehow the coach got a bunch of munchkins to preach to themselves the value of hard work. The chant helped them focus and listen to the coach. It also helped them believe in themselves. Hard work, usually such a negative concept, became an essential motivator in their game.

Just like these boys, sometimes I get distracted in my walk with God. My goal is to give God every area of my life, but it's always hard, and it requires work. Maybe you've dedicated your sexuality to God, but you find yourself distracted by a relationship, your feelings, your fears, or your friends. When this happens, you need a little coaching.

Paul's words from Philippians 3:12–14 serve as a good "hard work pays off" reminder for us. He had been beaten, betrayed, and put in prison for his faith. Before that he was a successful religious leader among the Pharisees. He had a long list of successes and failures, but he didn't focus on either of them. He worked hard to put all things behind him and focused instead on his prize. He understood that God deserved glory for each of his victories and that He had already saved him from all of his failures.

You will face times when you feel successful in your quest for sexual purity, and you will have times you feel like a failure. **The hard work pays off when you stop living for the approval of others and live for the glory of God**. It pays off when you are content being single because you know Jesus is sufficient to satisfy you. It pays off when you fully trust that God is guiding the steps of your life toward the right woman as you commit to becoming the right man. It's hard work to keep chasing after Jesus, but it pays off.

And the hard work of spiritual intimacy bears the fruit of sexual purity.

DAY 5

Pure by Position

God, create a clean heart for me and
renew a steadfast spirit within me.

—Psalm 51:10

Guys are wired to fight for position. I think the reason so many guys are drawn to certain things is because we internally want other people to notice us in the same way we notice others. I naturally notice successful people and winning teams. My attention is drawn to loud noises, shiny cars, big trucks—pretty much anything that stands out in its position. If it's prominent, guys tend to notice it.

As a Christian, you have to decide how you will fight for your personal and sexual purity. You essentially have two options: you can **fight for purity with your performance**. Or you can **fight for purity from your position**. Let me explain.

We are drawn to things that perform well. When a college football team begins slaughtering its opponents and wins a national championship, lots of "new fans" come out of the woodwork wearing the jerseys and the hats of the team that has the momentum. The better the team performs, the more fans they gain. The better their performance, the higher their prominence.

We often apply the same thinking to our own fight for purity. We tell ourselves that if we could just try harder and perform better, we would gain more victory in the areas where we struggle. Typically the harder we try to be perfect, the more discouraged we become when we fail or mess up.

A better approach is to **fight for purity from your position**. Instead of attempting to become pure by trying harder, you acknowledge that you are already pure in Christ because of His sacrifice on the cross for you. Your position is already secure. You are pure, holy, forgiven, and redeemed by His grace.

You are not fighting *for* a position of purity. You are fighting *from* a position of purity.

Jesus doesn't give us prominence based on our performance; He gives us a new position based on His perfection.

This simple truth can liberate you from the pressure of always trying to be perfect. You know it's impossible to be perfect, so see yourself from a new position. Jesus was perfect for you, and He offers you His perfection as a gift. This actually leads to greater purity overall.

I was adopted when I was just a few weeks old. My birth mother was fifteen when she gave birth to me, and she gave me to a family who could love and care for me. I always knew I was adopted, and my parents were clear that when I joined their family, I had all the rights and privileges as a member of that family. I gained a position in that family not based on my own actions but based on their decision. My position was secured by their decision.

Your position as a child of God was secured by His decision to die in your place and give you His salvation. Now all of your actions flow from that position of perfection. You are already pure, for-given, and clean.

pure by practice

How can a young man
keep his way pure?
By keeping Your word.

—Psalm 119:9

From elementary school all the way through high school, I enjoyed playing the three major sports: baseball, basketball, and football. I loved making tackles, hitting a double, and scoring a layup. I enjoyed blocking a noseguard, making the final out of the inning, and boxing out the biggest guy on the other team for a rebound. Those things were fun. And the louder the crowd cheered, the more I loved it!

One thing I didn't enjoy, though. Honestly, I hated practice.

Nothing seemed more useless to me than showing up at 3:15, as soon as school was out, and suiting up with all the other guys to go over offensive plays, defensive schemes, or to watch film of the next team we were going to face. It didn't help that practice was always when I was most sleepy and needed a nap. I despised practice!

But my coach was smarter than I. He knew that **practice preceded performance**. The way I performed during a game was a direct result of how I practiced before the game.

If you want to win the game, you have to practice before you play. The way you play is a reflection of how you practice.

There's a lesson here for you in the area of purity and relationships. Don't miss it.

Life is not a game. It's for real, and it matters for eternity. If you want to honor God with your body, with your relationships, and eventually with your marriage, you need to start practicing right now because the more you practice, the better you'll become.

I encourage you to begin "practicing purity" right now. Don't wait until you meet the woman of your dreams or until you're ready to get engaged. Practice purity here and now. Here are a few tips to get you started.

1. Ask an older Christian man to be your accountability partner. Your dad should be the first choice, but if he's not walking with God, ask a man at your church or your youth pastor. Confess sin and struggles to him. Be vulnerable.

2. Give God the first few moments of your day by reading Scripture and praying every morning before you go to school. It sets the tone for the rest of your day and places your mind on Christ, not lustful thoughts.

3. Sign up for a free filtering service for your phone, tablet, and laptop that will make it extremely difficult to look at porn. Try Covenant Eyes or XXX Church.

4. Avoid movies, TV shows, fitness magazines, and music that contain sexually charged images or words. These are triggers that take you places you don't want to go. Win the fight before it begins by cutting them off completely.

5. Decide now that you will not experiment sexually with a girl. Put it in writing and sign it. Give it to your parents, your pastor, or youth leader for accountability.

Practice isn't always fun, but it's sure to help you win the game.

DAY
7

pure by participation

And let us be concerned about one another in order to promote love and good works, not staying away from our worship meetings, as some habitually do, but encouraging each other, and all the more as you see the day drawing near.

—Hebrews 10:24–25

When my son Joseph was seven years old, he ended up playing football on a team with just eleven players, which is the bare minimum you need to even have a team. The boys ranged from kindergarten to second grade, and when the season began, I knew they would never win a game. I doubted if they would even score a touchdown.

But something happened about halfway through the season. They began to learn how to block and tackle and run plays. The more the coach worked with them, the better they became. They started playing as a team! They even won a game. Nobody was happier or more surprised than I was.

My son couldn't have won that game on his own against a team of eleven other players. He needed a team of guys around him to gain the victory.

The same thing is true in your battle for holiness. **It's a team effort, not an individual sport, so if you try to win all by yourself, you're guaranteeing your own defeat**. You're going to need people around you to help you win.

These people are called "the church." This is the body of Christ, the people who share your love for Jesus and your convictions and beliefs about life, money, salvation, and love. You need them to give you strength and support, encouragement and prayer. You also need them to be there for advice when you don't know what to do and wisdom when you've made a mistake and you feel dirty and ashamed.

To put it simply, **you walk in purity when you live in community.**

The brothers and sisters in the family of God create a safe place for you to learn how to resist temptation, confess your sin when you blow it, and watch how older men and women love and treat each other. The church is also where you sit under the teaching and preaching of God's Word and where your leaders instruct and correct you and show you what God says about how to live and work and serve others.

When you participate in the life of the church, you're immersing yourself in an atmosphere of good things and good people who will influence you to do good things and be a good person.

They will show you who Jesus is and whom you can become in Christ.

I am certain participating in church was integral in my fight for purity. I sat on the front row every Sunday and took notes when my pastor preached. I showed up early and stayed late whenever volunteers were needed. My own father was my Sunday school teacher for several years. I learned that I belonged to a larger family that loved and cared for me and wanted me to become a man of God. That reality made all the difference for me, and it can for you as well.

pure by planning

Don't those who plan evil go astray?
But those who plan good find
loyalty and faithfulness.

—Proverbs 14:22

I can sum up the main idea of this day in eleven short words: **If you want to be pure, you must have a plan.**

Without a plan to purity, you will fall flat on your face every time sin knocks on your door. Temptation is coming your way, ready to devour you and fill your life with regret and shame, so you need to be prepared to answer it when it arrives. **A solid plan devised ahead of time is better than a desperate prayer in the heat of the moment.**

The most effective way to combat sexual temptation, both as a single man and as a husband, is to employ three simple phrases.

1. Hate It. Make a decision that sin and temptation are not playthings to toy around with, but they are destructive forces that will fascinate you before they assassinate you. Choose to hate sin because of how it affects you and your relationship with Jesus. Choose to hate temptation because it will often give you enough momentary pleasure to stun you and then immediately switch up the rules and give you pain and regret you'll carry with you for years. Don't flirt with it. Hate it!

2. Starve It. The power of sexual sin grows stronger the more you feed it. Looking at porn, making out with your girlfriend, or listening to sexually charged music feeds that monster of lust. The best way to beat that monster is to cut off its food supply. Starve the sin! Stop feeding it. Break off the relationship with the girl. Ask your parents to cancel cable or satellite TV. Put filters on your devices. Replace those bad things with better things; become involved in a discipleship group at church. Begin a six-month devotional or a yearlong Bible reading plan. Start listening to sermons daily on iTunes or podcasts. Starve the sin, and start feeding your spirit.

3. Outsmart It. Think ahead and preempt the attack you know is coming. Make a decision never to be alone with a girl in the dark. Set a curfew with your parents so you're home before it gets too late to make good decisions. Commit to sexual abstinence until marriage and have an older brother in Christ stand with you as you begin dating. Don't ever hide relationships from your parents. Don't follow people on Twitter or be friends with people on Facebook who post images or links that will take you places you know you shouldn't go.

Come on, man! You're sharp, so don't act like a knucklehead. You know how strong sexual temptation is. Don't just stand there and wait until it attacks you. Get ready now. Learn from your past mistakes and create a game plan that you can put into practice when your hormones are raging. God will give you His strength, but you need to plan to stand against the sin when it comes knocking on your door.

DAY 9

pure in perspective

He predestined us to be adopted
through Jesus Christ for Himself,
according to His favor and will.

—EPHESIANS 1:5

You are not defined by your sin. You are defined by your Savior.

Because of Jesus and His love and sacrifice for you, the old version of you has died and been replaced with a new man; Jesus lives in you now. Adopt this new perspective, and you will see yourself not primarily as a hopeless sinner but as an image bearer of God, made for a purpose in His kingdom.

Perspective is everything. If you always see yourself as a typical young man with no real direction in life, then you will flounder around aimlessly without any idea of where your life is going. And if you see yourself as a dirty pervert who is covered in the guilt of your lustful thoughts or sexual sins, you will hide your face from God in fear, assuming He's angry at you and looking for a chance to punish you for your secret mistakes.

But there's a better way to see yourself. This perspective isn't based on your own good deeds or bad deeds. It's based on God's unconditional love for you. When you know you can never be pure without His help but that He took on your sin and made you clean by His death on the cross, you begin to see yourself from God's perspective: healed, forgiven, and new as His adopted son.

When I was in elementary school, I took a picture of myself and my parents to show-and-tell. I showed the picture of my family; then I told about how they adopted me when I was a young baby. I was proud to be adopted.

One of the boys in my class, who was a big bully and picked on all the other boys, spoke up and said, "You must have been a really ugly baby if your own mother didn't even want to keep you." He made me feel like an orphan that had been abandoned. His perspective made me feel unloved. Unwanted. Worthless. Discarded.

But when my mom picked me up after school, she changed my perspective. She could tell something was bothering me, and she asked what was wrong. I told her what the boy had said to me, that it made me feel like I didn't really belong in their family and that no one loved me. My mom said: "Don't listen to him. He doesn't know what he's taking about. His parents never got a choice, but your daddy and I did. We got to pick you out, like going to the pet store and picking out the cutest puppy there. When we saw you, we said, 'That's our boy! We want him!'"

My perspective changed after that day, and I never again doubted who I was or whom I belonged to. They chose me. Just as God chose you, loved you, and invited you into His family. Don't listen to any other voice. **You're pure because Jesus washed you clean when you became His.**

Appetite

The slacker craves, yet has nothing,
but the diligent is fully satisfied.

—Proverbs 13:4

It's easy for Christian guys to assume their appetite for sex is sinful, but that's just simply not true. God had a design in mind when He created guys and girls with a natural sexual appetite.

Have you ever wondered why you crave sex so much, but it seems like you have to wait so long to enjoy it? That's a natural way to look at sex as a Christian guy. You want it so bad, but you can't have it . . . yet!

So what is the purpose of your inner sexual appetite? Well, you actually desire sex for several really important reasons.

1. Procreation. Sex is the physical act that leads to children. For human life to continue and our species to avoid extinction, babies have to be born. In order for babies to be born, babies have to be made. You get the point.

2. Recreation. Sex is fun. It feels good. It's an enjoyable activity that should be mutually experienced by a man and woman within the covenant of marriage. It's so good, as a matter of fact, that married people actually keep doing it after the honeymoon. For decades. OK, enough about that.

3. Communication. Sexual intimacy is built on mutual trust between a husband and a wife. It's a means of communicating that trust, as well as the love and respect and affection the two spouses feel for each other. The two bodies act and respond to each other communicating deep commitment and vulnerability.

But like all appetites, just because you want it doesn't mean you should have it. All appetites must be controlled because an appetite without limits is a death sentence. Just imagine how quickly you would die if there were no legal limit to how fast you could drive your car! The desire to go fast has to be kept in check by a stronger authority like the Highway Patrol, or else every teenage boy would kill himself behind the wheel. And think about how sick we would all be if we ate anything we wanted, as soon as we wanted it, as much as we wanted, until we couldn't eat anymore. We'd all be morbidly obese.

Even though your appetite for sexual intimacy is not naturally sinful, keep in mind that your appetite is not innocent. You have a sinful, self-ish nature that doesn't like to wait when it craves something. That desire is kept in check by a stronger authority, the Holy Spirit. So to protect yourself from the consequences of immediately gratifying every sexual appetite you have, you must continuously, daily submit yourself to the lordship of Jesus Christ through prayer, Scripture, confession, repentance, and worship. The Spirit helps you control the craving now so you can one day fulfill your godly desire for sex with your wife for life.

Insecurity

Give thanks to the LORD, for He is good;
His faithful love endures forever.

—PSALM 107:1

Sin always causes us to struggle with insecurity because sin always causes us to question our identity.

When you have a lustful thought about a girl or when you watch a scene in a movie with way too much skin in it, you become insecure about God's love for you by wondering, *How could God keep loving me when I keep struggling with the same sin?* Or if you've ever gone too far sexually with a girl, you've probably asked yourself, *If I'm really a Christian, why couldn't I say no to that temptation? Maybe I'm not really a Christian after all. Or maybe I lost my salvation.*

Sin leads to insecurity. Just as Adam and Eve covered up their nakedness and hid from God after they broke His command and ate the forbidden fruit, we want to run and hide from God when we do something we know is wrong. At the root of this insecurity is a question: Does God still love me when I sin, or is He ashamed of me when I break His law?

The Bible tells us plainly that God's love endures forever and that when we sin, He is faithful to forgive us every time we repent. If you're a true Christian who has trusted Jesus alone for salvation and is still trusting Him daily, then you can never lose your salvation. Once you're adopted into the family of God, you will never be abandoned.

God keeps His promises. God completes His covenants. God finishes what He starts. When He began the work of salvation in you, He was starting a lifelong process that would take time and work and patience. He's invested a lot in you, so He won't expel you from His family when you fall or when you fail. He will keep transforming you.

Philippians 1:6 says, "I am sure of this, that He who started a good work in you will carry it on to completion until the day of Christ Jesus." This means you can replace your insecurity with full faith in God's ability to forgive you every time you sin because God is personally up to something in you. **He is building you into a man of God who reflects His glory as a witness to the world.** Your security isn't anchored in your ability to be pure. It's rooted in God's ability to love you in spite of your impurity, and by that love He purifies you completely.

In the ancient Greek and Roman world, when a child disgraced his family, the parents could legally "divorce and disown" that child, completely breaking ties and severing the relationship. But if a child had been adopted into a family, it was a permanent act that could never be undone or reversed. Parents could never disown a daughter or son whom they'd adopted. In the same way you're adopted into God's family, and He will never disown you.

When you doubt your ability, trust in His sufficiency. Remember that His grace is enough for you. You are secure because of your Savior.

DAY
12

Ego

I will boast in the LORD;
the humble will hear and be glad.

—PSALM 34:2

Psychologists define the ego as a sort of self-awareness of your own importance. Your ego is that part of you that feels its own self-worth, that enjoys being recognized and likes feeling pleasure.

Although it's necessary to know who you are and be acknowledged by those who love you, it's not healthy to think of yourself as the center of the universe. This is often how your ego works. It secretly whispers in your ear that you deserve a life filled with pleasure and that you should never deny yourself anything you want including sex, girls, and romance. The ego says, "If you want it, go ahead and take it because your desires are never wrong."

This was Satan's game plan when he tempted Jesus in the desert. Satan appealed to man's selfish desires when he promised all the kingdoms of the world if Jesus would just bow down to him. But Jesus had no selfish desires and no fallen nature, and He protected Himself through Scripture and being committed to God's plan.

Be aware of your natural tendency to feel like you should be able to take what you want. This includes relationships and sexual desires. **You**

live in a culture that will never encourage you to practice self-control. You won't ever watch a commercial that says, "Deny your hunger!" The messages you receive from advertising tell you to obey your urges, feed them when they arise, and go ahead and take whatever you want, no matter how much it costs or how it may affect you afterward. But you will pay a severe price when you live this way.

An unchecked ego will wreck lives because it never pauses to consider outcomes or consequences. It's only concerned with immediate gratification. God, however, cares about your future. He cares about your marriage, your kids, and your career, even before you have them. He wants something way better for you than a one-night stand or a cute, popular girlfriend for six months in high school.

The only way to combat the ego is to invite and welcome the transforming power of the Holy Spirit to be constantly changing you into a new man in Christ. As you morph into this new creation, you will notice that your goals will shift from taking what you want to praying for what God wants. **Your old desires will be replaced with a new desire to do what God desires.**

My absolute favorite Bible verse is John 3:30. John the Baptist (the cousin of Jesus) was telling his own followers about Christ. He was encouraging them to stop following him and start following Jesus because Jesus was the true Messiah. John says, "He must increase, but I must decrease." That's how you put your ego into its proper place. When you give Jesus the highest place in your life, your idea of your own self-importance will diminish as you keep making Him bigger and bigger.

Your life revolves around Jesus—so does the entire universe. It's not about you. It's about Him.

DAY 13

Flirt

Don't set foot on the path of the wicked;
don't proceed in the way of evil ones.
Avoid it; don't travel on it. Turn away
from it, and pass it by.

—PROVERBS 4:14–15

Remember this: you always flirt before you fall. So if you don't want to fall, don't flirt.

The first step toward sin is looking at the temptation long enough to justify it in your mind. **The longer you look, the more likely you are to linger; and the longer you linger, the more likely you are to lust.** Lust is a sinful craving to take something that's not yours to take—like sleeping with a girl who isn't your wife or fantasizing about sex with naked women on a screen to whom you are not married. They don't belong to you.

When you look, you linger. And the more you linger, the more you like what you see. This is flirting with sin.

When I think of a "flirt," I think of a guy or a girl who seems playful and fun, who gives the impression that they are interested in you without coming out and saying it clearly. A flirt is someone who is testing the waters. They want to see how far they can go.

Each of us tends to flirt with sin by getting as close as we can without actually doing it. The problem is that we're not satisfied with just getting close. We want to go all the way, and eventually we will. The key is to stop flirting in the first place.

Get away from temptation. Avoid it. You know where it will lead, so stay away. Because if you get too close, you will get burned.

My youngest son is obsessed with fire. He loves striking matches and lighting candles. This little pyromaniac would light a candle and sit and stare at it for ten minutes. Once, as he was watching the candle burn, I was watching him.

After a few minutes, he inched closer to the flame. It seemed to mesmerize him. Then a little closer. And a little closer. Finally, he reached out his little finger to the fire, feeling its heat. He pulled it back, but not too far, before he plunged his finger right into the middle of the flame.

Immediately he cried out in pain, jerked his entire arm backward, and starting wailing! He looked at me, his mouth wide open and his eyes filling with tears. I had observed the entire episode. I knew what was going to happen to him because it had happened to me before. I had warned him that he would be burned, but he wouldn't listen. He had to experience the pain for himself to believe it was real.

The funniest thing about that story was the look of sheer surprise on his face. We shouldn't be surprised when we get too close to sin and the sin hurts us. **Flirting leads to falling, and playing with sin leads to pain**. Stay as far away as you can. Listen to God's warning. Learn the easy way, not the hard way.

Follow

Carefully consider the path for your feet,
and all your ways will be established.

—Proverbs 4:26

A Chinese philosopher once said, "A journey of a thousand miles begins with a single step." You have the freedom to choose what kinds of steps you take and what direction you want to go because those small steps will eventually take you somewhere.

You can dabble your toes in the waters of sexual sin that will eventually drown you, or you can pursue purity by the power of the gospel and follow Jesus as His disciple. The choice is yours, but so are the consequences. It all depends on what you follow.

One of the most heartbreaking conversations I ever had was with a pastor who had been hiding some secret sins for years. He came to me broken after his wife had uncovered an affair he was having with a younger woman. As he shared his story with me, he confessed that he'd become addicted to pornography as a teenager. He would steal magazines from gas stations and hide movies from his parents. He thought getting married would fix his lust problem, but it didn't. He chose to follow this destructive pattern for years until porn didn't satisfy him. He wanted to act out his fantasies, and even though he had a wife and kids and a thriving ministry, he followed the pattern of secret sin until it caught up with him. When the truth came out about his affair, he lost his marriage and his ministry. He chose a direction, but he didn't get to choose the destination.

No one wants to end up like that, and you don't have to! If you follow God's wisdom and direction, that path will lead to a better destination. You won't arrive there by accident. You'll only get there by deliberately submitting yourself to the wisdom of Scripture and intentionally following Jesus instead of the pattern of this world.

Now consider the testimony of my dad. When he was ten years old, he gave his life to Jesus. He was a quiet and humble man, not a preacher or a pastor, just a blue-collar guy who worked with his hands and drove a pickup truck. He married my mom when she was still a teenager. He was dedicated to the church. He wrote his tithe check every Sunday and dropped it in the offering plate. He taught Sunday school for years, and I had the honor of sitting in his class for four years, listening to him teach me and a roomful of my friends. He quietly followed Jesus on a simple path of faithfulness.

He raised my brother and me and remained faithful to our mom until she died in 2010. He lived another eighteen months, fighting heart disease and diabetes. And the day before he died, he was sharing his testimony with his doctors and nurses in the hospital. I preached my father's funeral on Father's Day 2012.

He followed Jesus all the way to the end. That's how I want my life to end, following the same Jesus who saved me and made me clean. He is worth following.

Fall

You pushed me hard to make
me fall, but the LORD helped me.
The LORD is my strength and my song;
He has become my salvation.

—PSALM 118:13–14

When it comes to sin, fascination always comes before assassination.

You flirt with sin. You follow sin. You fall into sin.

But actually "fall into sin" may not be an accurate description because it sounds like an accident you never saw coming. If I said, "One day I was walking to class, and I fell into a huge hole beside the sidewalk," it would give the impression that I never saw the hole until I accidentally stepped in it. Sexual sin is similar to that hole because it lies in wait, oftentimes in places where you're not looking, and you seem to fall into it before you even know it's there.

Yet the reality is, you do know it's there. I am warning you. Maybe your pastor or your parents have warned you. The Bible warns you. The Holy Spirit warns you. Science and common sense warn you that sexual sin will bring consequences: regret, depression, guilt, disease, pregnancy, and emotional baggage. God has placed big, flashing warning signs all around the giant hole of sexual sin to keep you from falling into it. **Because He loves you, He wants to protect you.**

We always protect what we value, and God values you; He wants to protect you from a fall.

Before you fall into sin, you always follow the path of sin; and before you follow the path of sin, you flirt with sin. It all begins when you get curious. You wonder what it would feel like to go a little further with your girlfriend. You wonder what images would pop up on the screen if you typed in a few words on Google.

Curiosity brings you to the edge of something dangerous, and the closer you get, the more exciting it feels. But if you inch closer and closer to the edge, you'll eventually fall off the cliff. Once you fall, you realize the mistake. You see in hindsight how foolish you were to push the limits with that girl, to send those text messages, or to spend time on those websites.

In his book *Orthodoxy*, G. K. Chesterton paints a beautiful picture about the way God wants to protect His children from "falling" off the cliff into sin. He describes a scene on a mountaintop where a group of children are playing. Just a few feet away is a sheer cliff that drops straight off into a deep chasm. Anyone who falls from that ledge will surely die.

He poses the question: Are those children more happy and free playing on that mountaintop a few feet from the cliff, or are they more happy and free playing there with a fence to keep them safe from the danger of the fall? The answer is clear, isn't it?

Don't even flirt with sin. Stay behind the guard-rails God has placed there for your own joy and protection.

Forgiveness

If we confess our sins, He is faithful and righteous to forgive us our sins and to cleanse us from all unrighteousness.

—1 JOHN 1:9

The poet Alexander Pope once wrote, "To err is human; to forgive, divine." It is human nature to mess up and sin. But God's nature is to offer forgiveness to us when we fall.

The crazy thing is, when we do fall into sin, the thing we need to do is the last thing we want to do. We should run toward Jesus. We should immediately repent of our sin and turn to Him in humility. But instead we feel ashamed. In our embarrassment we try to hide what we did from Him, and we hide ourselves from Him. Just as Adam and Eve tried to run from God's presence after they disobeyed Him for the first time, our initial response is to run and hide. But this doesn't accomplish anything.

I saw this with both of my kids when they were in diapers. We were attempting to potty train them. They were getting older. It was our job as parents to prepare them for life, and part of that responsibility was making sure they matured past the stage where they carried around something gross and disgusting with them all day. But when we first began the process of getting them out of diapers, they both reacted with shame each time they failed to remember to go to the "big boy potty." They would hide in the corner of another room, sometimes even in a closet or behind the furniture, carrying their own mess with them, when all we wanted to do was clean them up.

We didn't want to punish our kids; we wanted to prepare them for life as young men, and we wanted to help them mature and develop. When they ran from us and hid in a closet, they were hiding from the people who wanted to help them.

In the same way, we all sin and feel ashamed when we disobey our heavenly Father. Our tendency is to run away and hide. But His desire is that we mature and develop into men of God that He can use in His kingdom. He doesn't want us to carry our sin around with us. He wants to purify us and to wash us with His grace. He does this through the blood of Jesus Christ that was shed on the cross on our behalf.

So when you fall, choose forgiveness instead of fear. Recognize that God already knows what you've done, and He is ready and willing to help you. He waits for you with His arms wide open.

Each time you approach God in prayer after you've fallen, you will experience His undeserved mercy, and each time you will grow in your understanding of how rich and deep His love for you truly is. The more you repent, the more you recognize: **your frailty is no match for His forgiveness**.

Fight

But thanks be to God, who gives us the
victory through our Lord Jesus Christ!

—1 Corinthians 15:57

We know Jesus has already fought the battle with sin and death, and He won the victory for us when He was raised from the dead. So why can't we defeat temptation? If Jesus fought and won, why do you so often feel like you're losing the battle against lust, peer pressure, and discouragement? Do you still have to fight for purity even though the gospel has already made you pure?

The simple answer is . . . *yes*. But the good news is: **you don't have to fight *for* victory. You can fight *from* victory**. Here's how it works.

When you get frustrated that you're still struggling with lust or depression or loneliness and you don't have the energy to fight those feelings, you remember that in Christ you have the power to overcome those feelings. You fight by focusing. You focus your thoughts away from the feelings, and you focus them toward Jesus. You fight back the temptation by focusing your eyes back to the source of your victory: Jesus Christ, risen from the grave and reigning over the entire universe! You are in Christ, and Christ lives in you so His victory over sin is *your* victory over sin. It's a different perspective on the fight for purity.

My grandpa fought in World War II. He was in the navy and was on an aircraft carrier in the South Pacific during the last half of the war. Halfway around the world, American troops were fighting the Nazis in France and Germany while my grandfather fought off the coast of Japan. Before he died, he told me an amazing story that nearly brought him to tears.

He was called to the deck along with the thousands of other men living on the ship. They all lined up in formation. The captain of the aircraft carrier announced to all of them that Hitler had taken his own life in Berlin and the Nazis had surrendered unconditionally. The war had ended in Europe! The Allies had fought, and they had won.

The war in Asia, however, still raged on. But the Allied forces were fighting with a renewed energy. They knew the war was essentially over, the Germans had surrendered, and Europe was spared from tyranny. It was just a matter of time before the war would end in the Pacific. *They were still in the fight, but their perspective had changed because their position had changed*. They belonged to the victors. Now they were fighting *for* victory *from* victory.

This reflects the reality of how we fight for purity.

Yes, you must fight for purity. But you fight from a position of victory. You know the war has been won. It's just a matter of time before Jesus returns to the world He created and restores all of creation. You have victory "now" but the full effects are "not yet."

When you're frustrated, fight by focusing on the war that was won on the cross. It will give you faith to keep fighting.

Flee

Run from sexual immorality! "Every sin
a person can commit is outside the body."
On the contrary, the person who is sexually
immoral sins against his own body.

—1 CORINTHIANS 6:18

The best way to fight sin is to flee temptation.

Run from it. Get away. Don't look at it. Don't consider it. Don't flirt with it. Flee! The reason this strategy is so effective is simple: you are not strong enough to fight sexual sin and temptation in your own power. It would be the same as attempting to hold up your hand and scream "STOP!" to a hurricane or a tsunami.

Here are a few tips on how effectively to flee a situation before you fall.

1. Pursue something better. If you're already running after Jesus, turning away from the attempts of the enemy to distract you with the promise of sinful pleasure will be easier. One of the basic laws of physics says that an object in motion will stay in motion unless an outside force acts on it. If you're already moving toward God, then you have momentum in your favor, and you'll be more likely to keep moving in His direction when the outside force of temptation comes knocking on your door.

2. Plan ahead. You've probably heard the saying, "Those who fail to plan are planning to fail."

This applies to our battle for purity. Have a plan in place to flee anything that would tempt you to compromise your faith in Jesus or your standards in relationships. Set a curfew with your parents. Put a filtering service on all your devices. Write out your values and standards for relationships and share them with your mentor, your parents, or your pastor. Implement the plan now so you can flee anything that violates it later.

3. Prepare your heart. Proverbs 4:23 says, "Guard your heart above all else, for it is the source of life." Temptation always grabs us at the heart level, promising us something we crave or desire, so we must guard our hearts by preparing them. How do we prepare our hearts? By giving Jesus the highest place, by making Jesus the center, by placing Jesus on the throne of our hearts. You will be prepared to flee sexual sin when you have developed the holy habits of giving Jesus the firstfruits of your life: praying daily on your knees in His presence; reading and meditating on His precepts in Scripture; worshipping Him privately and corporately through hymns, choruses, and psalms; and listening to His voice throughout your day as He guides you and convicts you and encourages you.

4. Purpose your mind. Don't become a mental couch potato when it comes to temptation. Think through what you will do in times of tempting. When you get a text or an e-mail that looks fishy, delete it before opening it. If someone flirts with you and you know it will lead to trouble, cut off the conversation immediately. Read reviews of movies to find out if there's nudity before agreeing to go with your friends. Don't be mentally passive. Engage your mind in this battle so you can flee when the time comes.

And just remember that every time you flee temptation, you are running toward something even better.

DAY 19

Refuse

Though the lips of the forbidden woman drip honey and her words are smoother than oil, in the end she's as bitter as wormwood and as sharp as a double-edged sword.

—Proverbs 5:3–4

I had a natural attraction to her. It was pure chemistry. She was physically beautiful, and I liked that little feeling in my stomach when I first saw her. I knew I was in trouble though because we would never work out in a relationship together. My heart was hooked, but the Holy Spirit was screaming at me, a warning of the danger I was about to get myself into if I didn't walk away. I had to refuse to give in to the natural attraction.

I honestly believe I could have fallen in love with her if I had pursued her. However, **just because you are in love with someone doesn't mean that's the person you should marry.** You can fall in love with the wrong person. You can fall in love with someone who is totally wrong for you, who doesn't believe as you do, or who is going a totally different direction in life than you are.

I knew I could say yes, but this meant I'd be breaking my word and three of my commitments to God.

1. First, I would be dating a girl who wasn't a Christian. No matter how attracted I was to her personality or her outer beauty, things would

end badly between us if we didn't share my most basic conviction about the person of Jesus Christ.

2. Not only had I committed to refuse all relationships with non-Christians, but I had also dedicated my life to ministry as a teenager. This led me to a commitment only to marry a woman who, like me, was called to ministry. If I wasn't willing to marry a woman who wasn't called to ministry, then why would I consider dating one?

3. I had no doubt in my mind that a relationship with this girl would eventually lead to sexual sin. I came to grips with the hard truth that you are just more naturally attracted to some people, but that alone is no reason to commit the rest of your life to them. Sex and emotional chemistry are not foundations you can build a marriage on. It takes trust, faith, service, and sacrifice.

The choice I had is the same choice you will face in your sexual decisions. The situation may be different, but the heart issue is the same. Whom will you choose, and whom will you refuse?

Ephesians 5:3, 6–8 says, "But sexual immorality and any impurity or greed should not even be heard of among you. . . . Let no one deceive you with empty arguments. . . . Do not become their partners. For you were once darkness, but now you are light in the Lord. Walk as children of light."

Here's the raw truth. The quest for sexual purity is dependent on whom you choose. But it also depends on whom you choose to refuse. Every time you refuse something *now*, you are actually choosing something *then*. Every *no* today allows you to say a better *yes* tomorrow.

DAY
20

Reject

Her house is the road to Sheol,
descending to the chambers of death.

—Proverbs 7:27

I want you to take about five minutes and read Proverbs 7. Then read it again. Then a third time.

Without a doubt, it's the boldest and clearest passage in the Bible regarding sexual sin. Every guy should memorize the whole chapter.

The big idea in Proverbs 7 is simple: a man of God must reject all thoughts and temptations to indulge in sexual sin. It's a stern warning. If you don't, bad things will happen.

> She seduces him with her persistent pleading;
> she lures with her flattering talk.
> He follows her impulsively
> like an ox going to the slaughter,
> like a deer bounding toward a trap
> until an arrow pierces its liver,
> like a bird darting into a snare—
> he doesn't know it will cost him his life.
> Now, my sons, listen to me,
> and pay attention to the words of my mouth.
> Don't let your heart turn aside to her ways;
> don't stray onto her paths.
> For she has brought many down to death;
> her victims are countless. (Proverbs 7:21–26)

Does that sound like a girl you want to know better?

The man who wrote those words wasn't playing around. He uses disturbing, violent language to describe what happens to a guy when he allows himself to become entangled in a sexual relationship with a woman who is not his wife. **These cautions are more than symbolic language.** They are horrifying, frightening warnings of a deadly plot that can ruin your life through the portal of momentary sexual pleasure.

And you know intuitively that those words are true. You may have a friend who got caught up in a relationship with a girl, and before you knew it, he was like a different person. You watched him change before your very eyes. That's because sexual sin has the power to overtake you and control you unlike any other sin. It looks so enticing, and it feels so good . . . for a moment. But the end result is slaughter, the grave, and death.

If you know this is the outcome, the only logical approach you can take is utterly and completely to reject every message the culture sends you promising pleasure through sex. Reject the commercials that glamorize a secret affair. Reject the lyrics in that song that glorifies an illicit encounter with a girl. Reject the text message you know contains a picture of a girl in a sexually provocative pose. Reject the thought of clicking on that link on your iPad because on the other end of that link is *more* than a pretty girl with no clothes on. There's a snare waiting for you, and once you step into that trap, it will be harder than you ever imagined to get free from it.

Sin takes you farther than you want to go. It keeps you longer than you want to stay. And it costs you more than you want to pay. Be smart and see the outcome before you head down that road. You've been warned.

DAY
21

Redirect

The one who walks with the wise
will become wise, but a companion
of fools will suffer harm.

—Proverbs 13:20

My father died way too early. He was only sixty-nine and could have lived a lot longer if he had practiced a healthier lifestyle. When he passed away, my wife and I began changing many of our daily habits, including what we ate. I realized that I loved eating crunchy things: chips, crackers, and cookies. A friend told us we needed to learn to **redirect our desire** to eat those foods by eating something that was actually healthy as well as crunchy. So we started eating almonds. It only took a few days to develop a new habit, but it started by redirecting our desire for crunchy foods.

Your desire for intimacy and love is not an evil desire, but it can lead to destructive choices if it's not redirected. Just as I redirected my craving for crunchy junk food, you can redirect your craving for a relationship to a better destination. And in turn, your decision will prepare you for marriage where you can enjoy guilt-free sexual intimacy along with sacrificial love.

God has hardwired you to connect with other people, not just to have sex. You need friendships:

guys you can hang out with and older men who can give you advice, tell you stories of their own failures and successes, and coach you through tough seasons. You also need females in your life: a mom, a sister, aunts and grandmothers, and friends at church and school. You need to learn how to relate to women, how to understand them, and how to value them as your sisters in Christ. Simply put, you need to be around people, and you need to belong to people in order to become the kind of man God wants you to be.

Redirect your desire for a girlfriend and romantic love by focusing on the other relationships you need to be involved in at this point in your life. Walk with wise people, and you'll grow wise.

Reject the cultural stereotype that paints you as a mindless, sex-crazed teenage boy who only thinks about how to get a girl into bed. Redirect your need for human connection to healthy relationships with your pastor, your parents, your coaches and teachers, and even your grandparents.

By the age of forty, I had lost all four of my grandparents and both my parents. I am so glad that when I was a teenager, I wasn't so obsessed with chasing girls that I ignored the important relationships with my own family. Even though they are all with the Lord now, I had strong relationships with them while they were alive. I am now reaping the benefits of those relationships as I practice what I learned from them every day as a dad, husband, leader, and pastor. Their wisdom made me wiser, and you can only absorb others' wisdom by spending time with them in real relationships.

DAY
22

Redefine

Help me stay on the path
of Your commands, for I take
pleasure in it. Turn my heart to Your
decrees and not to material gain.

—Psalm 119:35–36

Don't define happiness the way the world does, but see it as anchored in your relationship with God.

Your culture defines happiness as the accumulation of things, the pursuit of personal pleasure, the gaining of popularity and influence, and relationships that make you feel good about yourself. These definitions are completely wrong.

You need to redefine what true happiness is. Reject what Hollywood, society, and the media tell you. God's Word says you should turn your heart away from selfish gain because you can only find true delight when you walk in the path God lays before you. This verse from Psalms cuts against the grain of everything you will ever hear about finding a meaningful life, especially in the area of girls and sex.

To be a Christian guy in this culture means you are swimming upstream against a rushing current of temptation and selfishness. Girls are viewed as sex symbols. Dating is viewed as a doorway to having your sexual desires fulfilled. A group of girls recently told me that at their school the rule for dating was simple: "Put out or get out!" Guys automatically expected a girl to do things for them on a first date that only a wife should do for her husband. They all felt objectified and hopeless.

I encourage you to reject completely the assumptions many guys make about relationships and redefine what kind of man you want to be, what kind of marriage you want to have, what kind of family you want to raise, and what true happiness actually is.

Just as the gospel defines your purity, the gospel also defines what constitutes real happiness in relationships. The gospel tells you that you were redeemed from your sin by the loving sacrifice of Jesus on the cross. The gospel tells you that a woman will never satisfy your deepest desires. Only Jesus can do that. The gospel tells you that sexual intimacy is not primarily about your wife serving you and making you happy, but instead it's about you loving and cherishing your wife as your partner, not your plaything or your sex toy. The gospel tells you that the world's way of defining happiness is wrong, that it won't last, and that it won't sustain you throughout the storms and struggles of your life.

The gospel redefines everything. It tells you that you are loved and accepted by God's grace. It tells you that you don't have to perform, be cool, act tough, or conquer anything to be loved unconditionally. And it tells you that you have Jesus Christ as an example, showing you how to love and treat others, including the woman you will eventually marry.

Don't believe the hype. Don't buy the lies. **Happiness is redefined by the gospel, and it's rooted not in finding the right person to marry but in becoming the kind of man God could trust with one of His daughters.**

Refocus

I have chosen the way of truth; I have set Your ordinances before me. I cling to Your decrees; LORD, do not put me to shame. I pursue the way of Your commands, for You broaden my understanding.

—PSALM 119:30–32

When you're discouraged because you're single or lonely, read what God says to you in His Word; let it give you strength.

These verses from Psalm 119 can encourage you to refocus your thoughts on God and His truth in times when you feel no one is out there for you. I know how that feels.

From the time I was about eight years old, I dreamed of getting married. By the time I was in my late teens and early twenties, I was so ready to get married that I wondered every time I met a cute Christian girl if she was my future wife and if we were going to have a family. The longer I waited, the more discouraged I felt. But every time I started to doubt God's ability to bring me a wife, I grabbed my Bible and read a passage of Scripture. Just a few verses made all the difference, and it reminded me that my hope was not in a girlfriend or a wife. My hope had always been in Christ alone, and that is where I needed to refocus my desires and my dreams for love and intimacy.

Have you noticed that when you're trying to do your homework or study for a test, you automatically get distracted by a thousand little things? None of them are related to what you should be focusing on. They're not important. Yet you find yourself checking Facebook or posting a picture on Instagram or texting a friend or watching a dumb video on YouTube. When you realize you've wasted fifteen minutes by being distracted, what do you have to do to get back to work?

You have to refocus. You remind yourself what you need to do. Here are a few things I do to help me get back on track, and they all require action.

1. Turn off anything that makes a distracting sound.
2. Sit up straight and blink my eyes a few times.
3. Take a few deep breaths and force myself to think about the task at hand.
4. Walk outside, breathe some fresh air, and get back to work.
5. Talk to myself out loud and say, "Clayton, you need to refocus on finishing this. Clear your mind of all distractions. You're not getting up until you're finished."

You have to **choose** the way of truth. You must **set** your heart on His laws. You must **hold fast** to His statutes and **run** in the paths of His commands. These are verbs. These are actions. They require effort, but the effort pays off in the long run so don't give up. Just learn to refocus.

DAY 24

Recommit

I called to the LORD in distress;
the LORD answered me and
put me in a spacious place.

—PSALM 118:5

I want to share a little trick with you I believe will help you when you find yourself in a situation where you think you may do something you will eventually regret.

When you're close to giving in to a sexual temptation, declare out loud that you belong to Jesus and you need His help. Audibly ask the Holy Spirit to come to you and get you out of that situation. Crying out to God is extremely powerful and tangible.

When I start feeling the desire to look at porn or have lustful thoughts, I close my eyes, I open my mouth, and I say out loud, **"Here and now, Lord Jesus, I recommit myself to You as my Lord and King. Help me resist the temptation to do anything that would dishonor You."** I am not kidding when I tell you this works.

I travel for a living. I am constantly in places where temptations are at my fingertips. I pass a strip club every time I drive to the airport. I stay in hotel rooms where I could rent pornographic movies. I have a laptop I could easily use to access millions of websites with sexual images.

What keeps me from giving in? Am I some kind of supernatural Christian with special powers?

Absolutely not. I am a sinful and weak man, just like you. I have the same moments of weakness you have. And you and I are no different from any of the great men of the Bible: King David, Samson, Peter, Noah, and Moses. They all fell into some sort of temptation because they were normal men like us.

Honestly, the only thing sometimes that has kept me from giving in to the curiosity of what lies on the other side of that remote control in the hotel room is the ten-second declaration I make, out loud, when I recommit myself to the lordship of Jesus Christ.

Just like this verse from Psalm 118, it feels like pure distress when you have an opportunity to commit sexual sin. But read that verse again and notice what it says: "I called to the LORD in distress; the LORD answered me and put me in a spacious place." He answers and sets you free. Do you see that? That's exactly what you should do when you're feeling overwhelmed.

When you feel the frustration of wanting to have sex, look at porn, masturbate, or hook up with a girl for selfish reasons, cry out to God. Do it loudly! And when you call on Him for help, remember this verse and expect Him to do the same thing for you. Believe that He will answer you and that He will set you free from the situation, that He will deliver you from the temptation, and that your recommitment to Him as the true source of all joy and peace will make you stronger to face the next temptation.

DAY
25

Remember

Only be on your guard and diligently
watch yourselves, so that you don't
forget the things your eyes have
seen and so that they don't slip
from your mind as long as you live.

—Deuteronomy 4:9

Did you know that the easiest way to replace your doubts is by remembering?

When you begin to throw a pity party for yourself because you don't have a girlfriend or when you begin to compare yourself to all the other guys who have tons of cute girls around them all the time, you need to replace that negative attitude. The best way to do that is to remember all that God has already done for you.

- Remember how He rescued you from your sin and saved you.
- Remember all the times He has bailed you out of bad situations.
- Remember all the prayers you've prayed that He has graciously answered.
- Remember how He has provided for your needs before.
- Remember how He has taken care of things that you had no control over.
- Remember how faithful He has been to you, your family, your church, and your friends.

God's past faithfulness is an indication of His future provision. When you begin to recall all the amazing things God has done in your life, you will find yourself encouraged about how He will provide for you in the future.

So instead of getting hysterical, you need to get historical. Learning to remember is a spiritual discipline like prayer, worship, and tithing. It's easy to suffer from spiritual amnesia. We are quick to forget the numerous times and ways God has come through for us.

Don't you think if God was kind enough and powerful enough to provide you with forgiveness of sin, a new heart, the promise of heaven, the presence of His Holy Spirit, and the guarantee of eternal life, that He is more than able to provide you with a lovely woman you can marry and spend your life with?

If you are getting frustrated because you haven't found her yet, remember that God is smarter than you, and He knows when you are ready for a relationship.

If you are growing impatient in your fight for sexual purity while you watch so many of your friends, in real life and on social media, brag and gloat about all their girlfriends and parties, remember that God offers you something better than temporary pleasure.

If you are about to give up your virginity to a girl you really believe you're in love with, remember that God has a plan for your love, and it is in the covenant and commitment of marriage. Love is not a license to do whatever you feel like doing.

If you feel dirty, ashamed, and condemned because of a past sin you can't seem to forget, remember that God offers forgiveness for every sin we commit when we repent of that sin, turn away from it, and turn to Him alone for mercy and restoration.

Sometimes the most practical thing you can do in your fight for purity is to remember all that God has promised you and all that God has done for you. **When you remember what He's done, you gain the courage you need to do what you must do.**

Replace

How happy is the man who does not follow the advice of the wicked or take the path of sinners or join a group of mockers! Instead, his delight is in the LORD's instruction, and he meditates on it day and night. He is like a tree planted beside streams of water that bears its fruit in season.

—PSALM 1:1–3

You may need to replace the things and people who tempt you with better, more godly objects of affection. Think about how something as small as ending a bad relationship could completely turn your life around emotionally and spiritually. Imagine how a few small replacements could set you up for victory over temptation!

These verses from Psalm 1 sound spiritual, but they're actually filled with perhaps the most practical commonsense advice a young man could ever hope to hear once he decides to commit his life and his body to the lordship of Christ. This passage is all about replacing bad influences in your life with good ones. It challenges us seriously to consider what kinds of voices we are allowing to speak to us and what kind of people we are allowing to influence us.

We all know that our minds slowly, gradually, eventually begin to think like the people we spend time with. But it's more than that. We fill our lives with other voices too.

1. Social media. Stop following people on Twitter who constantly tweet mean, sarcastic, or hurtful things. Unfollow someone as soon as they retweet or like anything that is sexually tempting. Don't click links on someone's Facebook page you think may lead you to a bad place. Be cautious when scrolling through someone's Instagram feed, and make up your mind beforehand that you will not view images that don't glorify God.

2. Movies and TV. Ask yourself what kinds of messages you are subconsciously ingesting from the reality shows you are watching or the movies you rent. Ask your parents to cancel their subscription to HBO, Cinemax, and Showtime because you know the programming on those channels will lead you to sin. Stop watching trash filled with stupid adolescent drama. It makes you dumber by the minute.

3. Close friends. You may need to replace your closest friends with some new ones. If they're influencing you to compromise your purity, rethink your convictions, or hide your actions from your parents, then you need new friends. Stop worrying about being mean, and start worrying about your testimony and your own soul. Walk away. Delete their numbers from your phone.

When our family decided to stop drinking soda, we didn't stop drinking altogether—drinking is necessary for life. If the body is not hydrated, it ceases to function. We simply replaced the objects that were tempting us (Coke and Dr. Pepper) with better things that would benefit us and make us healthier (water and tea).

You don't have to stop having friends, watching TV, or participating in social media. You just need to make good choices about what kinds of voices and influences you will remove from your life and what better voices and influences you will replace them with. Don't deliberately choose to submit yourself to the influence of mockers and fools. Replace them with wise, godly influences.

DAY
27

Repent

If you return, I will restore you.

—JEREMIAH 15:19

Don't you wish you had a time machine you could climb in as soon as you mess up? You could just push a button, rewind about twenty minutes, and make a better choice—the one you should have made twenty minutes earlier, because you know the sin you committed didn't deliver on its promise to satisfy you. It felt good for a minute; then you felt guilty. Or dirty. Or angry. Sadly there's no such thing as a time machine because it's scientifically impossible for us to go back in time.

But God has given us something much better than a time machine. Because He created the universe (including time and space), He is not bound by time. What He did for you two thousand years ago—when He sent Jesus to die on the cross in your place for the forgiveness of your sins—is applied to you today even though you still mess up. And it's just as powerful and real today as it was over two millennia ago when Jesus was crucified outside the city gates of Jerusalem.

The way we access this kind of power is not by going back in time because **you cannot unsin** no matter how much you wish you could. **But you can repent.**

Repent means to "turn away and turn around." Think of it as seeing the sin you just committed, recognizing it was wrong, then turning your head away from it, looking the other way, almost like looking at something gross and disgusting makes you want to turn your gaze in another direction. This is the first step in repentance.

Then you go a step further. You actually turn around and go the other way. Think of it like driving down the road looking for a restaurant where you'll meet your family for dinner; then you realize the restaurant is the other way, the opposite direction. You've been driving the wrong way so you turn around. You make a U-turn and head the other way. That is the second step in repentance. You turn away from the sin. You turn around and head the other direction, away from the sin and temptation and toward God's grace and forgiveness.

Here are some practical ways you can make repentance a holy habit in your fight for purity.

FOR GUYS

1. As soon as you have a lustful thought or act on a sinful desire, tell Jesus. Pray about it immediately and don't delay. The longer you wait, the harder it will be to repent.
2. Read, meditate on, and memorize Scripture that assures you of God's willingness to forgive you.
3. Confess your sin to a trusted brother in Christ that you respect.
4. Keep a journal where you write out your prayers of repentance and the verses that help you receive mercy.
5. Remember the process of repentance the next time you're tempted with the same sin as a way to avoid the same outcome.

When you practice repentance, you lose the need for a time machine, and you may just grow a little stronger in your faith along the way.

DAY 28

Receive

If God is for us, who is against us? He did not even spare His own Son but offered Him up for us all; how will He not also with Him grant us everything?

—ROMANS 8:31–32

One of the most effective ways Satan destroys the joy in a Christian's life is to convince you and me that God stops loving us when we sin. Our own insecurity makes us vulnerable to these kinds of feelings.

"If you were really a Christian, you wouldn't have a desire to look at porn."

"If you really love God, why do you keep having lustful thoughts about that girl at school?"

"If God really heard your prayers, He would give you the strength to stop masturbating, especially since you've prayed for Him to help you."

"You're not trying hard enough to be pure. You're lazy and a pathetic example of a true follower of Christ."

I've fallen for every one of these lies before, and I'm guessing you have too. So how do you move past these kinds of condemning thoughts and emotions?

You focus more on Jesus and less on you. You understand that you are not pure by being perfect. You are not pure by how you perform. You are pure because of your position in Christ, as a beloved child of God who has received His grace before and who still needs to receive it now.

Remember this: salvation cannot be achieved; it can only be received. It's a gift God offers you, and you can only receive it when you believe it.

Apply this to your purity. You know how impossible it is to win the battle against all the forces of sexual sin on your own. You need God's strength in your weakness. **Your purity cannot be achieved; it can only be received, and it is received when you believe!**

- You believe God cares about what you do with your body because your body is His home, where His Holy Spirit lives.
- You believe God has set standards and rules governing relationships and sex that are not there to hurt you but to help you and bless you.
- You believe God hates sexual sin, not because He is an angry God but because He loves you, wants what's best for you, and cannot stand to watch you suffer the consequences of your sin.

- You believe God is holy, that He has made you holy through Jesus Christ, and that you must fight for holiness from a place of total trust in His ability to give you power over lust and loneliness.

When you believe all that God has said, you can receive all that God has done. It's much easier to pursue a life of purity when you approach each day as an opportunity to receive more of God's power and grace that day instead of trying (and failing) to be pure on your own. If you could receive His salvation as a gift you didn't earn, you can also receive His power to forgive you when you sin and give you victory over temptation and condemnation when you fall.

DAY
29

Attention

Trust in the LORD with all your heart, and
do not rely on your own understanding.

—PROVERBS 3:5

When I was taking my driver's test at age fifteen, I was so excited finally to get my license that I made a critical error. I was talking to the DMV employee who was giving me the test, and as we drove, I approached a stoplight. It was green so I stopped paying attention to oncoming traffic and attempted to make a left-hand turn at the intersection. But because I wasn't paying attention, I didn't see the truck driving through the red light. It nearly hit us. It would have been my fault. We barely escaped a head-on collision because I stopped paying attention. I was so focused on the payoff (getting a license) that I forgot the process (taking the test).

But the process is what gets you to the payoff. Where you look will determine what you long for, so place your attention on godly things. What catches your eye will enter your heart so pay attention to where you look. **Paying attention is the art of thinking about what you want your future to be like and asking yourself if your current actions will get you there**.

As you dream about getting married and as you imagine what it will be like to enjoy sex and physical intimacy with your wife, make sure you are not so enamored with the payoff that you forget about how important the process is right now of becoming a man of character. Here are some steps you can take in the meantime to keep your attention focused on becoming a man of God.

1. Get involved at your church. Show up early and stay late. Volunteer to do things you wouldn't normally do. Clean up after church meals. Help with children's church.

2. Consume all the good teaching and preaching you can. Sit on the front row with a pen and a notebook when your pastor is preaching. Download sermons from pastors you know and trust, and read solid books by great Christian authors that will keep your mind and heart focused on spiritual formation.

3. Honor your parents. Treat them with love and respect. Listen to what they tell you to do; then do it without complaint. Observe how they live together and serve each other. Pay attention because you will one day be doing the same thing.

4. Finish tasks. Don't be lazy and apathetic. When you start a project, whether at school or at home, make sure you do it with excellence. Realize you are forming habits today that will follow you into tomorrow, and those habits will be there in greater force when you get married.

5. Make two lists: one with all the characteristics of the kind of girl you want to marry and one with all of the characteristics you want to possess as a husband. **Happiness doesn't come from finding the right person. It comes from being the right person, and that will require your paying attention.**

As John Galsworthy said, "If you do not think about your future, you will not have one."

Affection

Love the LORD your God
with all your heart, with all
your soul, and with all your strength.

—DEUTERONOMY 6:5

You crave what you consume so change your affections through worship, serving, and obedience to God.

Affection is a funny thing. It's a feeling, a force that draws you to a person or a thing. You could easily define *affection* as "the feeling of desiring, craving, or wanting something." But another aspect to affection is essential in your lifelong battle for purity.

Affection is closely tied to attention. Here's how it works.

Whatever you give your attention to will also get your affection. The thing you look at, admire, obsess over, think about, dream about, talk about, wish for, and fantasize about is the thing you will begin to love. So if you fill your eyes and your brain with images of naked women or lustful images, you will crave those thoughts more strongly and more often, eventually craving the real thing, then eventually going after the real thing and giving in to the temptation. What gets your attention will eventually get your affection.

So the key is to desire, crave, and want good things. You can learn how to place your affection on the things of God, and it starts by taking small steps that may seem hard but are really easy once you begin.

Deuteronomy 6:5 instructs us to love God with all we've got. That means we give Him all of our affection. This starts by filling your mind with things that make you think about God. It means reflecting on the death of Christ on the cross. It means reading Scripture, placing it in conspicuous places where you can see it all throughout the day. The more you consume the things of God, the more you will crave the things of God and the less you will crave sin. You are replacing affection for the world with affection for your heavenly Father. When you do that, you will create positive and uplifting thoughts about things that are praiseworthy.

Your brain and your heart can be trained by constant use. You can teach your brain what to think about and your heart what to love, but it takes discipline and consistency to get your affections right.

When I was in high school and college, I struggled with an overwhelming desire to have sex. I knew that if I ever started, I would probably never stop, so I had to train my mind to stop fantasizing about sex all the time. I wrote Bible verses on three-by-five-inch cards and placed them on my dashboard, my mirror, and all over my room. Almost everywhere I looked, I was being reminded of how great God is and how much He loves me. A crazy thing happened: after a while, I noticed that I felt greater love and affection for God and less temptation to sin sexually.

I consumed godly things, and the more I consumed, the more I craved.

DAY
31

Intention

You open Your hand and satisfy
the desire of every living thing.

—Psalm 145:16

Be intentional by practicing the daily habit of telling yourself the kind of person you want to be and the kind of person you want to marry.

When you understand that you need to pay attention to the voice of God by placing your attention on the things of God, you can begin giving your affection to God by loving Him with all your heart, soul, mind, and strength. What gets your attention will gain your affection. But following the path of purity as a disciple of Jesus will also require a steady, intentional pursuit of God's presence in your life.

One big lesson I learned when I started dating my wife, Sharie, was that after a few months in the relationship, when the newness wore off and the infatuation died down, I had to make a deliberate effort to spend time with her. I learned a brand-new word. I had to become "intentional." I had to think about things ahead of time. I had to plan our time together. I had to plan special occasions, dates to certain restaurants, and get-togethers at my house when friends would come over to hang out with us.

What she helped me understand was simple: if I didn't plan anything specific for us, then we would never spend time together doing meaningful things or having meaningful conversations. We would never get to know each other by just hanging out, which just led to watching TV or some other royal waste of time. When we became intentional about taking our dating relationship to the next level of engagement and then toward marriage, we noticed that we felt more confident and secure in our relationship because of the time we had spent intentionally getting to know each other.

When you get intentional about your relationship with Jesus instead of being spiritually lazy, you will notice that you will become more secure in His love. This will make you more confident as a man of God and will help you fight from your position of purity that you already have in Christ.

Here's a short list of ways you can live intentionally for the glory of God:

1. Honor your parents when they set a curfew for you. If they don't set a time for you to be

home at night, set your own curfew, and ask your parents or a friend to make sure you keep it. You are less likely to mess around or mess up with a girl if you are home early.

2. Write down a specific list of the lines you will not cross with a girl physically and keep it tucked in your Bible. Read over it and review it every day when you read your Bible. Let God remind you of His desire for your holiness.

3. Don't have a TV, a laptop, an iPad, or even your own smartphone in your room alone with you at night. You know bad things happen when you have all access and no accountability so be intentional and limit your access to temptation.

Daily, intentional steps toward God will always lead you in the right direction.

DAY 32

Insecurity

The Lord is faithful in all His
words and gracious in all His actions.

—Psalm 145:13

Have you ever watched a chain smoker? He'll pop the box against his hand until one lucky cigarette peeps out of the bottom. Two fingers bring the cigarette up to his mouth while, simultaneously, the other hand reaches for the lighter. He flicks the wheel, inhales the red flames into the end of the cigarette, and a puff comes out of his mouth. In only a few minutes, the cigarette has burned to the nub.

And before the nub is fully extinguished in one hand, the other hand already has the box of new smokes ready. It's time to repeat the process.

Sometimes I sit and listen to guys talk about the long list of girls who have never given them what they need. Each breakup leaves them dissatisfied and disillusioned. They don't know who they are as young men or what kind of men they want to be. And before their hearts are healed, their eyes are already looking for the next girl who will change it all.

It's time to repeat the process. Like a chain smoker.

Chain dating is as destructive as chain smoking. Sure, smoking can kill your body, but chain dating creates a chasm of insecurity in your soul as it eats away your identity.

But if chain dating makes people miserable, what makes it so addictive?

You were originally designed to find absolute fulfillment in your relationship with God, but that fellowship was messed up in the garden of Eden. The passion you have to find love and security is designed primarily to lead you to a relationship with Jesus and secondarily to share life with your wife. Unfortunately in our impatience we try to fill the emptiness in our hearts with one girl after another.

Some of my worst relationship decisions were made on the rebound out of insecurity. I didn't give my hurting heart time to heal from the last girl before I started flirting with the next one. Boom! Suddenly a new girl came along to distract me before I could realize the danger of my addiction.

Chain dating originates from a need to find something other than God to fill our needs. So it only makes sense that nothing other than the presence of God can defeat the effects of this addiction in our lives. We have to stop looking for a girl to satisfy us and start backing up our faith with action.

I know it will take faith to believe that He really sees you and loves you. I know it will take trust to believe He will satisfy you. But here is my challenge: take a break from girls for a while, and watch God meet your needs. I'm not saying it will be easy, but every guy I know who has done this and stuck with it has become more secure and confident in himself and in his relationship with God. I know this will be true for you too.

Inspection

There is a way that seems right to
a man, but its end is the way to death.

—Proverbs 14:12

Allow the Holy Spirit to speak to you, convict you, and inspect your heart and your mind on a daily basis.

Anytime you ask a guy's advice about dating, love, or sex, and he tells you to "just trust your heart," you need to ignore that advice and him because he is dead wrong. The worst thing you can do is trust your heart because your heart— like mine—is a wicked, selfish thing that desires momentary pleasure with no regard for the glory of God.

Instead of trusting our hearts to tell us what to do in romantic relationships, we need to invite the Holy Spirit to inspect our hearts. What *we think* is right and good may lead to death in the end according to Proverbs 14:12. For this reason we must ask, beg, implore, and pray for God to shine His bright inspection light down into our souls and reveal things to us that we are too blind to see.

All guys tend to think of themselves at times as way more awesome than they really are. We need someone to bring us back down to earth and give us a dose of reality. Who better than God to reveal to us the hidden sins we may be unaware of in our own hearts?

The Holy Spirit is the perfect inspector. Like any inspector His job is to dig deep into the dark places where no one ever goes. He traces things back to their origins. He leaves no stone unturned. He knows exactly where to look and exactly what to look for, and if anything is wrong or out of place, He will warn you by convicting you of that sin and making you aware that things aren't right.

When our family built our home a few years ago, we were not allowed to move into the house and live there until the county inspector came out and walked through the house, around the house, in and out of the house, and under the house. He grabbed and pushed and pulled and jerked on things. He moved things around and looked behind objects. He tested wiring and plumbing and construction. He checked everything to make sure we would be safe moving into the house.

That's exactly what the Holy Spirit does for you. He's the inspector. He pushes and pulls and kicks things around to uncover anything in you that may be wrong, unsafe, sinful, or destructive. He does it because He loves you and wants what is best for you. He doesn't want you injured or hurt, so inviting Him to inspect your heart is one of the wisest things you could ever do.

Let your prayer be that of the psalmist: "Search me, God, and know my heart; test me and know my concerns. See if there is any offensive way in me; lead me in the everlasting way" (Psalm 139:23–24).

Comparisons

Run from sexual immorality! "Every sin a person can commit is outside the body." On the contrary, the person who is sexually immoral sins against his own body. Don't you know that your body is a sanctuary of the Holy Spirit who is in you, whom you have from God? You are not your own, for you were bought at a price. Therefore glorify God in your body.

—1 Corinthians 6:18–20

Most guys create their own list of what is acceptable and unacceptable when it comes to the girls they date. Interestingly enough, the standards aren't set in stone and will change the longer they are with a girl. In fact, sometimes their standards change according to "how far" the girl had gone with her last boyfriend.

A lot of Christian guys ask me, "How far is too far?"

"I've touched a girl's breasts, but we didn't have sex."

"I've kissed a girl, and we took our shirts off, but we didn't get totally naked."

"I've had oral sex but definitely not intercourse so I'm still good since I'm a virgin."

"We take naps together and make out in bed or on the couch, but we're not going all the way."

Some guys want a solid answer so they can draw a line in the sand, a protective barrier to keep sin far away. Others are hoping my answer will be vague so they can do whatever they want without truly crossing the line. For example, if I were to say, "Don't have sex before marriage," they may think that means they can participate in a variety of intimate pleasures with their girlfriend without actually going "all the way."

But the goal in dedicating your sexuality to God is to avoid both legalism and abusive grace. To do this you have to let go of your comparisons. Forget "the list." Don't compare your actions to others. Don't let your girlfriend dictate your intimacy standards. If you're truly allowing the gospel to define your purity, the most important person to consider is God. And the verse above is pretty clear on what He thinks about it.

How you treat your body is not about what other guys are doing or what your girlfriend says is OK. How you treat your body is about what you believe about your body. When you became a Christian, God decided your body was the perfect place for Him to live. You became a temple; a place for the Holy Spirit to occupy. God moved in.

So let me ask you a question: "How far is too far?"

- **How far is too far** for you to go in dedicating your body and your sexuality to a God who died to give you life?

- **How far is too far** for you to start seeing your sexuality as part of your testimony, part of the gospel story in your life?
- **How far is too far** to stop comparing your sexual behavior with the actions of your friends and instead start dedicating your behavior to the God who lives inside you?

Who's with me? Let's lay down the lists and stop the comparisons.

DAY
35

Expectations

How can a young man keep his way pure? By keeping Your word. I have sought You with all my heart; don't let me wander from Your commands. I have treasured Your word in my heart so that I may not sin against You.

—Psalm 119:9–11

Before I was married, I dated because:

- I wanted to make new friends.
- I was afraid to be alone.
- I thought I would be a good influence on her relationship with Jesus.
- She was fun to be around.
- I needed a date for a dance, a prom, or an event.
- I thought it was God's will.

We date for many reasons. I had a relatively mild dating experience with few regrets. Still, like most people, I have a few I wish I could wash away. But instead I think I'd take my "dating self" out for coffee and say: "Clayton, you wouldn't believe the amazing love story God has planned for you. But, if you'd like to avoid some heartache along the way, you need to sit down right now and decide what kind of girl you're looking for. Do you want a girl who encourages your faith or one who is embarrassed by your love for Jesus? Do you want her to share your commitment to purity, or are you going to choose someone who wants to push the boundaries? Do you want a best friend or a fling? Set your expectations now because most relationship mistakes originate from a lack of vision."

You must decide what kind of person you are looking for before you start looking. Ask God to help you set a list of expectations. Expectations are your first line of protection against compromise.

Maybe you think having expectations is intolerant, rigid, and unkind. But if you ordered spaghetti at a restaurant and you got a slab of salmon instead, you'd probably send it back. If you interviewed for a position as a finance director but had a degree in psychology, they'd probably choose someone else. If a pro football team kept losing, they'd fire the coach and find someone who could get the job done.

Living a sexually pure life is not easy. If you want to stay on this narrow path, if you want to glorify Jesus as His child, you have to set some expectations to make it work. Here are some expectations you should have according to Psalm 119.

You and your potential girlfriend should both be:

- Living according to God's Word
- Seeking God with all your hearts
- Open and willing for God to keep you from sin
- Learning the Word of God so you can live by it

These are essential and foundational to setting the right goals and creating a healthy list of wise expectations. Now take some time to set some personal ones and give your list to God in prayer.

DAY
36

Grow Up

Then we will no longer be little children, tossed by the waves and blown around by every wind of teaching, by human cunning with cleverness in the techniques of deceit. But speaking the truth in love, let us grow in every way into Him who is the head—Christ.

—EPHESIANS 4:14–15

Maturity is not about age; it's about the acceptance of responsibility as God places opportunity before you.

Rick Warren, a pastor and author, once said something so wise that I still think about it on a regular basis when I am struggling in my relationship with a friend or my wife. He said that after thirty years of marriage counseling with couples, he could sum up the basic advice every couple needed to hear as the source of a majority of their marital issues: "Grow up."

So many of our temptations and frustrations come from simply not getting our way. We have an idea of what we want, and we can't stand it when we don't get it. This is acceptable behavior for an infant and even for a toddler. But parents begin at an early age teaching tiny children that they aren't the center of the universe and that they cannot always get what they want. God is our Father, and He wants to teach you this lesson as His son.

According to Ephesians 4, **immaturity leads to inconsistency**. When you lack maturity, you are tossed around emotionally like a ship being blown around by strong winds. I know you've felt that way because I constantly struggled with inconsistent feelings as a young man, especially with girls. I couldn't decide which girl I liked, or I felt conflicted because I was no longer attracted to the girl I once liked and I didn't know how to tell her. How could I like two or three girls at once? And on top of that, I felt like a pagan because I wanted to have sex with all of them, even though I knew it was off-limits. I felt like a "relationship schizophrenic."

An older man in my life had the courage to "speak the truth in love" to me. His words were painful at the time, even offensive, but they cut through my pride and touched my heart. He said, "A time comes when the little boy needs to sit down, and the grown man needs to stand up. Now is that time."

Now is that time for you too. **Pursue maturity—not the natural process of getting older but the spiritual process of going deeper.** Leave childish things behind. Move on to accept the responsibility of becoming a man of God, the kind of man who knows how to walk with Christ, respect women, say no to worldly desires, cherish the Scriptures, love the church, work with excellence, and finish what he starts.

By God's grace you can grow up and become a man after God's own heart.

DAY
37

Give Up

You took off your former way of life,
the old self that is corrupted by deceitful
desires; you are being renewed in the spirit
of your minds; you put on the new self,
the one created according to God's likeness
in righteousness and purity of the truth.

—EPHESIANS 4:22–24

Joy is not found in trying harder but in surrendering more to the lordship of Jesus Christ on a daily basis.

These verses in Ephesians tell us that we were created to be like God in His righteousness and purity. If that's the case, how do you get there? You probably want to be righteous, but you don't *feel* righteous. And purity is a lofty goal, but it's a lot harder to be pure when you're surrounded by impure images and temptations and thoughts all the time.

The way you get there is by giving up your former way of life, your old way of thinking about things, your former way of doing things. Paul says in Ephesians 4, "You took off" your old self. Consider the old you as dead, done away with, replaced with a new man that has been made new by Christ. Give up the old mind-set, the old perspectives on girls and sex and love. Embrace the new you that Jesus has empowered you to be.

When you give up the old you, you rise up to become the new you. It's a fruitless labor to keep trying harder to be holy on your own. You'll just get frustrated. And what usually happens when you get tired of trying? You give up, right? Right! That's what I want you to do. Give up!

Give up trying to be perfect.

Give up the constant battle with guilt and shame when you fail and fall.

Give up trying to defeat temptation in your own power.

As you "take off" your old self and give up that old way of thinking and living, you can "put on the new self" that was created to be holy and pure. You can rise up to become the man God has empowered you to be.

Rise up to your true identity in Jesus Christ.

Rise up to the challenge of becoming a man of virtue and integrity.

Rise up to the opportunity to go deeper in your walk with Jesus through prayer and His Word.

Rise up to the responsibility of honoring women and treating them as your sisters in Christ.

Rise up to holiness by turning your eyes and your heart away from evil things.

When Jesus takes control of your life, He changes you from the inside out. It may seem like a slow process, but He is making you new every day. Don't fight that process. Surrender to it. Give up and give in to God as He gives you His holiness and makes you pure by the power of His gospel.

DAY 38

open up

A thief comes only to steal and to kill and to destroy. I have come so that they may have life and have it in abundance.

—John 10:10

Satan's goal is to use your sin to separate you from the love of God. Let me show you how he tricks us all.

If you have a past full of regrets and mistakes . . .

- He lies to you and tells you that you will never measure up.
- He tells you that you will never be pure or accepted because you can never again measure up to God's standards or other people's expectations.
- He tells you that you might as well give up and give in to sin because you'll never succeed in anything holy or righteous.
- He tells you that you'll never be able to change so you decide to live it up, hoping God will cover it up later when it's time to pay up.
- He uses your feelings of inadequacy to keep you from knowing God's unconditional love and acceptance.

If you've lived a (comparatively) mild life of sin . . .

- He tries to find whatever glaring sin you are trying to hide.
- He pinpoints your weak spot, hammering you with condemnation until you feel unworthy and useless to God.
- He tells you to give up or to begin working your fingers to the bone to make up for your inadequacies.
- He uses your feelings of shame to keep you from knowing God's unconditional grace and acceptance.

Satan is no fool. He has been using the same lies on God's children for generations. Sadly we often absorb his lies into our emotions. They feel so familiar to us that they have become part of our theology of who God is. The enemy will do anything to keep us from a healthy relationship with God.

But God has also been speaking a message to His children for generations. His message to you is much more encouraging so **open up your heart and receive what He says to you!**

That is, in Christ, God was reconciling the world to Himself, not counting their trespasses against them, and He has committed the message of reconciliation to us.

—2 Corinthians 5:19

Therefore, if anyone is in Christ, he is a new creation; old things have passed away, and look, new things have come.

—2 Corinthians 5:17

Do not remember the past events, pay no attention to things of old.

Look, I am about to do something new; even now it is coming. Do you not see it?

Indeed, I will make a way in the wilderness, rivers in the desert.

—Isaiah 43:18–19

Did you hear Him? Stop looking at your past and living in your past! One day all the things you can't bear will become beautiful. God has begun a beautiful work in your heart of redeeming and restoring you for His own pleasure and purpose.

God sees you as a brand-new person so leave the regret of your past mistakes behind and start believing that you are who God says you are, regardless of the lies Satan throws in your face. **Open up your heart to all God has for you and wants to do in you and through you.**

DAY 39

Pray Up

Take the helmet of salvation, and the sword of the Spirit, which is God's word. Pray at all times in the Spirit with every prayer and request, and stay alert in this with all perseverance and intercession for all the saints.

—Ephesians 6:17–18

The greatest weapon you have at your disposal in your fight for purity is the ability to call on God in prayer and know He hears you. He will enable you to have victory over temptation, fear, loneliness, discouragement, and shame.

I learned if I pray when I feel tempted, immediately I sense God's strength. Just that split-second reaction of calling on God in the moment of weakness refocuses my mind onto Jesus and away from the bad thoughts I struggle with.

Here are some Scriptures you should pray in times of testing. And if you pray them often enough, you will eventually memorize them, and they will be hidden in your heart to the point that you will find yourself automatically praying these verses when you are weak . . . without even thinking about it. They all come from the book of James, written by the brother of Jesus Himself.

> A man who endures trials is blessed, because when he passes the test he will receive the crown of life that God has promised to those who love Him.
>
> —James 1:12

Consider it great joy, my brothers, whenever you experience various trials, knowing that the testing of your faith produces endurance. But endurance must do its complete work, so that you may be mature and complete, lacking nothing.

—James 1:2–4

Is anyone among you suffering? He should pray. Is anyone cheerful? He should sing praises.

—James 5:13

Therefore, confess your sins to one another and pray for one another, so that you may be healed. The urgent request of a righteous person is very powerful in its effect.

—James 5:16

Now if any of you lacks wisdom, he should ask God, who gives to all generously and without criticizing, and it will be given to him. But let him ask in faith without doubting. For the doubter is like the surging sea, driven and tossed by the wind.

> —James 1:5–6

Therefore, submit to God. But resist the Devil, and he will flee from you. Draw near to God, and He will draw near to you. Cleanse your hands, sinners, and purify your hearts, double-minded people!

> —James 4:7–8

Humble yourselves before the Lord, and He will exalt you.

> —James 4:10

No one undergoing a trial should say, "I am being tempted by God." For God is not tempted by evil, and He Himself doesn't tempt anyone. But each person is tempted when he is drawn away and enticed by his own evil desires. Then after desire has conceived, it gives birth to sin, and when sin is fully grown, it gives birth to death.

—James 1:13–15

Who is wise and has understanding among you? He should show his works by good conduct with wisdom's gentleness.

—James 3:13

But the wisdom from above is first pure, then peace-loving, gentle, compliant, full of mercy and good fruits, without favoritism and hypocrisy.

—James 3:17

But be doers of the word and not hearers only, deceiving yourselves.

—James 1:22

Arming your heart and mind with these Scriptures will help you as you fight the battle for purity. They will remind you that God is right there with you, and He is on your side.

DAY
40

Don't Give Up

Everything is possible
to the one who believes.

—MARK 9:23

I've had a relationship with Jesus since I was fourteen years old. I've tried to live a life that glorified Him, but looking back, I know I missed the mark sometimes. My mistakes have served me as valuable learning experiences.

Jesus' disciples had their own learning experiences. In one of them a desperate father asked them to help his son who was possessed by a spirit. The spirit made the boy mute, often tried to throw him into fire, and threw his body to the ground where he would foam at the mouth and gnash his teeth. Jesus had given His disciples the power to heal and cast out spirits, but for some reason they couldn't do it this time. The teachers of the law pounced on the disciples' "failure," using it as an opportunity to attack the disciples with theological arguments.

When Jesus showed up, the chaos continued as the boy convulsed and fell to the ground foaming at the mouth. But instead of focusing on the boy, Jesus tried to pull the father's faith to the surface. Caught in panic mode, the only words this desperate father could muster were, "If You can do anything, have compassion on us and help us" (Mark 9:22).

Jesus confounded the chaos with one clear statement: "'If You can'? Everything is possible to the one who believes" (Mark 9:23).

When Jesus said this, the boy's father confessed, "I do believe! Help my unbelief" (Mark 9:24).

Jesus heard the honest words of a father: "I want to believe You can heal him, but I'm having trouble. Can You help me believe? Will You give me the faith so that my child can be free?" Jesus responded by delivering the boy.

Sometimes your faith is hiding beneath your confusion and doubt. Maybe you believe it's impossible to be sexually pure again. Perhaps you've felt like a failure for so long that you don't believe you deserve a good marriage or the unconditional love of a wife. Whatever your doubts, I plead with you: *don't give up!*

Everything is possible for one who believes.

When I lack the faith to believe, I cry to God, "I believe! Help my unbelief."

When I was in the eighth grade, I gave Jesus my sin, and He gave me salvation. I committed my body to Him as my total and complete Lord and Master, and I wrote down my commitment to Him. I kept it in my Bible alongside the list of the qualities I wanted in a wife. During high school and college, I had difficulty at times staying focused on Jesus. I wanted sex so bad. I wanted love so bad. I wanted to get married so bad! But by God's grace I didn't give up.

Today I am married to my best friend. I have two awesome sons. And Jesus is sweeter and more precious to me than He was when I first met Him.

So no matter how much you mess up, don't give up! It is worth the fight. Stay faithful and humble, and God will provide your every need in Christ Jesus.

About the Author

Clayton King is president of Clayton King Ministries and Crossroads Summer Camps, the teaching pastor at Newspring Church, and campus pastor at Liberty University. He is an evangelist, author, and missionary. Clayton began preaching at the age of fourteen and has traveled to thirty-six countries and forty-six states. He's written nine books and preached to more than three million people. Clayton is passionate about seeing people far from God repent of their sin and begin a relationship with Jesus. He loves to pastor pastors and empower Christians for ministry. He also loves four-wheelers, action figures, black coffee, and his wife and two sons.

For more information on Clayton and Sharie, their speaking ministry, or Crossroads Missions and Summer Camps as well as free sermons and resources, visit www.claytonking.com and www. sharieking.com.

YOU NEED COURAGE

TO LIVE FOR GOD.

TO FAITHFULLY LEAD YOUR GENERATION.

Courageous Teens is a student-focused presentation of *Courageous Living* by Michael Catt, senior pastor of Sherwood Baptist Church and executive producer of the hit film COURAGEOUS.

Catt brings fresh insight to "stories of people in the Bible who displayed great courage when it would have been easier to play it safe . . . (who) challenge me to keep moving forward. They demand that I examine my priorities and deal with anything that brings fear to my heart."

Teen readers will be inspired to resolve to live for God as they learn more about Abraham, Moses, Nehemiah, Ruth, Daniel, and many more.

Best-selling youth market author Amy Parker arranges the heart-stirring material into four categories: Courageous Faith, Courageous Leadership, Courageous Priorities, and Courageous Influence. Discussion questions are also included at the end of each chapter.

What if the focus of your life wasn't about you?

The Big Picture is a gospel-centered book for teenagers and young adults that tells the story of the God who has always been with man and, through his Son and Spirit, always will. Best-selling authors Hayley and Michael DiMarco guide readers to be more aware of God's presence with us today and better sense His call for us to make disciples of all nations.

The gospel didn't begin in the New Testament. It was there, "In the beginning," at the genesis of everything. Across the whole of human history, God's grand narrative of love and redemption has been unfolding, a love gloriously displayed at the cross. This is the story of Jesus, and all history and Scripture point us to this good news.

Teenagers live in a world defined by pressure—and with no shortage of opinions on how they should handle it. In *The Big Picture*, teens will develop a bigger perspective of Scripture and how the story of Jesus Christ ties it all together and how He should be our main focus. Nothing brings life into focus like the gospel!

Every WORD matters™
BHPublishingGroup.com